REAL REVOLUTIONARIES

THE REAL
BENEDICT
ARNOLD
THE TRUTH BEHIND THE LEGEND

by Jessica Gunderson

Content Consultant:
Richard Bell
Associate Professor of History
University of Maryland, College Park

COMPASS POINT BOOKS
a capstone imprint

Real Revolutionaries is published by Compass Point Books,
1710 Roe Crest Drive, North Mankato, Minnesota 56003
www.capstonepub.com

**Library of Congress Cataloging-in-Publication data is available on the Library of Congress
website.**
Names: Gunderson, Jessica, author.
Title: The Real Benedict Arnold : The Truth Behind the Legend / Jessica Gunderson.
Description: North Mankato, MN : Compass Point Books, a Capstone imprint, 2020. |
Series: Real Revolutionaries | Audience: Grade 7 to 8.
Identifiers: LCCN 2019014609 (print) | LCCN 2019016110 (ebook) |
ISBN 9780756558970 (eBook PDF) | ISBN 9780756558925
Subjects: LCSH: Arnold, Benedict, 1741–1801—Juvenile literature. | American loyalists—
Biography—Juvenile literature. | Generals—United States—Biography—Juvenile literature. |
United States. Continental Army—Biography—Juvenile literature. | United States—History—
Revolution, 1775–1783—Juvenile literature.
Classification: LCC E278.A7 (ebook) | LCC E278.A7 G865 2020 (print) |
DDC 973.3/82092 [B]—dc23
LC record available at https://lccn.loc.gov/2019014609

Editorial Credits
Mandy Robbins, editor; Sarah Bennett, designer; Eric Gohl, media researcher; Kathy McColley,
production specialist

Photo Credits
Alamy: Artokoloro Quint Lox Limited, 16, Hum Images, 38, Niday Picture Library, 31, Pictorial
Press Ltd, 15, The Print Collector, 7; Granger: 9; Library of Congress: 20, 50; The New York
Public Library: 35, 48–49; Newscom: Prisma/Album, 25; North Wind Picture Archives: cover,
1, 11, 28, 40–41, 45, 49 (top), 54; Shutterstock: Everett Historical, 57, Raymond B. Summers, 13;
Wikimedia: Americasroof, 42, Public Domain, 47

Design Elements
Shutterstock

All internet sites appearing in back matter were available and accurate when this book was sent to
press.

Printed and bound in the USA

PA71

Contents

CHAPTER ONE
AN ACCOMPLISHED TRAITOR

*B*enedict Arnold's name has come to mean *traitor*. He was a turncoat and a spy. After his betrayal, the mere mention of him caused Americans to turn away in disgust. But he wasn't always a traitor. He was a brilliant general who led the young Continental military to many victories before he switched to the British side. He was a complicated man—intelligent, troubled, ambitious, greedy, and misunderstood.

In the spring of 1775, in the early days of the Revolutionary War (1775–1783), Benedict Arnold enlisted in the American Continental Army. Throughout the war, he commanded troops and strategized many victorious battles. But, despite his skills, he was often overlooked for promotions. Then, in October 1777, Arnold was badly injured at the Battle of Breymann's Redoubt. His leg nearly had to be taken off.

Arnold could no longer serve on the battlefield. The following year he was sent to Philadelphia as military governor. There, he spent his earnings wastefully and found himself in debt. Many of his friends were loyalists—on the side of the British.

As the war dragged on, he felt more and more unhappy with the way the Continental military treated him and his successes. He no longer had faith in the rebel cause. In 1779, he heard that the British were making offers for Continental officers to switch sides. If he went to the side of the British, he would receive a reward. He would also remain a general, but in the British army. It was an offer he couldn't refuse. Arnold accepted, a decision that would shape his legacy forever.

A MOTIVATED YOUTH

Before he became a turncoat, Benedict Arnold had many accomplishments, beginning in his youth. As a boy, he was an ambitious and intelligent student. Born to a wealthy family on January 14, 1741, Arnold grew up with privilege. His father was a successful merchant in Norwich, Connecticut, selling goods around the world. His family's wealth allowed young Benedict to attend private boarding school. He excelled at many subjects, especially Latin and math. His goal was to eventually move on to Yale University. But by the time he was 12 years old, everything had changed. Three of his four siblings had died of disease. His mother fell into depression, and his father fell into the bottle, drinking away his earnings. As the family fell into debt, Benedict Arnold had to drop out of private school. His hopes of attending Yale were dashed.

In 1755, at age 14, Arnold became an apprentice for the Lathrops. The Lathrops were relatives who owned an apothecary shop that made and sold medicine. Ever ambitious, Arnold learned all he could about running a successful business. Over the next few years, the Lathrops came to treat Arnold like their own son. They admired his hard work and intelligence, and they sent him on trading voyages to the West Indies and London. On these travels, he learned sailing skills and how to negotiate business deals.

A SUCCESSFUL BUSINESSMAN

Arnold's success as a student and apprentice led him to become a profitable business owner. Arnold's mother died in 1759. After her death, Arnold's father started drinking even more heavily. He died in 1761, leaving young Benedict with a burden of debt and the care of his younger sister, Hannah.

Benedict Arnold owned an apothecary shop such as the one depicted in this image.

Arnold was determined to rebuild his family's wealth and reputation. He sold the family home to pay off the debt. The Lathrops gave him a small sum of money to start his own business. Arnold left Norwich for New Haven, Connecticut, where he could start fresh.

New Haven was a booming port city on Long Island Sound. Arnold opened a small apothecary shop. But he didn't sell only medicine. He also sold books and other goods. Selling a variety of items at his store made his shop very popular. As his business grew, he moved the store to a larger space near New Haven's harbor.

Then he set his sights on the sea. In 1764, Arnold formed a partnership with Adam Babcock, another New Haven merchant. The partners bought a merchant vessel. The following year they bought two more. They sailed north to Canada and south to the West Indies, trading goods such as rum, molasses, grain, and timber. Arnold's business ventures were a success. By the mid–1760s, Arnold was one of the most successful businessmen in New Haven. But something was happening that would threaten Arnold's business—British taxation.

The decade before, the French and Indian War (1756–1763) had taken place between the British and the French. The war was largely fought over land holdings on the North American continent. In 1753, small skirmishes between the two country's militias broke out. War was officially declared in 1756. Many American colonists fought in the war on the side of the British. In 1763, the war ended in a British victory. The French gave up all North American possessions. But the British were also left with a large war debt. The British Parliament decided to tax the American colonists to help pay off the debt.

The new tax acts, such as the Sugar Act of 1764, affected Benedict Arnold's business. The Sugar Act required that certain goods could only be sold to Great Britain. This made trading less profitable. Trade floundered. The following year, the Stamp Act of 1765 required that an expensive stamp be placed on all printed documents. Colonists had no representation in British Parliament, so they had no say in the tax laws. Arnold, like many colonists, was angered by this.

American colonists in Boston protested the taxes that led to the Revolutionary War. They hung likenesses of British officers.

British tax laws caused the economy in the colonies to plummet. Benedict Arnold's business struggled. By 1767, he was nearly bankrupt. But Arnold was a wise and talented businessman. He expanded his range of goods and began selling cattle and hardwoods. Eventually he was able to pay his debts and save money. By the early 1770s, Benedict Arnold was once again one of the most successful businessmen in New Haven.

SKILLED MILITARY STRATEGIST

Another of Benedict Arnold's skills was his keen military strategy and foresight. In 1774, with war looming, a patriot group called the Sons of Liberty began organizing militia units across the colonies. Arnold had no military training, but in late 1774, he organized a militia unit in New Haven called the Second Company Connecticut Governor's Foot Guards. Arnold led the unit in military drills on New Haven Green. In March 1775, the unit voted on who would become their captain. They chose Benedict Arnold.

Arnold's first success as a military leader came just shortly after he was elected captain. In April 1775, the Foot Guards marched to Cambridge, Massachusetts, where colonial militia were gathering. Along the way, Arnold learned that the militia was in desperate need of weapons and ammunition. An idea formed in his mind. Fort Ticonderoga, on the banks of Lake Champlain in

New York, had a stockpile of weapons. The fort was also only lightly guarded by the British.

When he reached Cambridge, Arnold told his superiors of his plan. They approved the plan and promoted him to colonel.

Arnold organized the militia and set off for Fort Ticonderoga. When he reached the Massachusetts border, he learned some troubling news. Ethan Allen, leader of the Green Mountain Boys militia, was also planning an attack on the fort. The Green Mountain Boys were only a few miles away from Fort Ticonderoga, ready to attack without official orders.

The French built Fort Ticonderoga between 1755 and 1759. The British attacked and took control of the fort in 1759.

Arnold put assistants in charge of his troops and quickly rode north, 12 miles (19 kilometers) over mountains and muddy terrain. He finally caught up with Ethan Allen and the Green Mountain Boys in a tavern near Castleton, in present-day Vermont. When he showed them his official orders to lead the attack, the Boys shrugged him off. They informed him they would only follow Ethan Allen, or they would go home. Arnold knew the Green Mountain Boys would be an asset to the attack. He reluctantly agreed to share the leadership with Allen.

In the early hours of May 10, 1775, Arnold, Allen, and about 300 militiamen gathered at Hand's Cove on the shores of Lake Champlain, ready to slip across the lake to the inlet below the fort. But there weren't enough boats to carry them all. About 80 men crossed, and the boats were rowed back to gather the others. Time ticked on, and the rest of the men didn't arrive. As dawn approached, Arnold and Allen knew they couldn't wait any longer if they wanted to surprise the sleeping British. They charged ahead with only a quarter of their militia.

As Arnold had predicted, Fort Ticonderoga was only lightly guarded. The patriots stormed in, rousing sleeping soldiers and seizing their weapons. The commanding

The success of the capture of Fort Ticonderoga depended on the element of surprise. The sleeping British weren't prepared for an invasion.

officer surrendered the fort without hesitation. The seizure of Fort Ticonderoga was the first offensive action the Continental Army took against the British.

About a week later, Arnold took the offensive one step further. Without orders to do so, he gathered his men and sailed across Lake Champlain to the British outpost of Fort St. Jean, Canada. There, he and his men again surprised the British, commandeering weapons and capturing an important warship, the *George*, which Arnold renamed the *Enterprise*.

Another instance that highlighted Arnold's strategic mind was the Battle of Valcour Island. In October 1776, Arnold predicted that British General Guy Tarleton would sail an invading force down Lake Champlain, hoping to regain control of Fort Ticonderoga and Crown Point. He had to come up with a plan to stop them.

As the British approached, Arnold positioned a fleet of warships on a small channel between Valcour Island and the western shore of Lake Champlain. Then they waited. On October 11, the British fleet approached. The channel was so narrow that the British would need to sail their ships in single file. The Continental army surprised the British. Furious fighting ensued until nightfall. The British ships far outnumbered the Continental ships, and Arnold realized his small fleet would be defeated if fighting continued

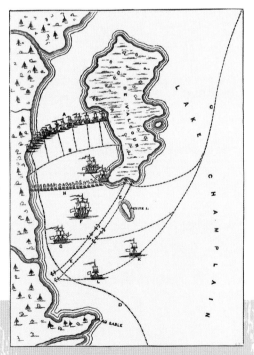

The British drew up plans that ultimately failed to defeat Benedict Arnold's forces on Lake Champlain.

another day. Arnold commanded his ships to flee under the cover of night. When the British chased them, Arnold ordered his troops to set fire to the warships so they couldn't be seized.

Arnold's strategy stalled the British advance. Winter was coming, and the British knew Lake Champlain would soon freeze over. So the British turned back to Canada. Their plan to invade New York was delayed until spring.

Arnold's accomplishments early in the war had strategic importance. The capture of the forts on Lake Champlain effectively cut off communication between the British north of New York and those stationed in more southern locations. His strategies helped build a strong Continental presence in the north.

INSPIRING LEADER

Benedict Arnold was not only a keen military strategist, he was also a dedicated leader who inspired his troops. He never wanted to give up, despite all odds. His men looked up to him and admired his determination. One such instance was the harrowing trek to Quebec in the late months of 1775.

In the summer of 1775, George Washington was named commander-in-chief of the Continental Army. One of Washington's goals was to invade Canada and attack the British force there. One idea was to invade Canada from two directions—one from Lake Champlain to Montreal, the other through the Maine wilderness to Quebec City. In August, Benedict Arnold met with Washington and offered to lead the trek through Maine. Arnold was familiar with the area from his trading voyages there.

Arnold hastily prepared for the expedition. He interviewed troops, searching for those who could endure a 350-mile (563-km) march through heavily wooded, unsettled land. He also ordered the construction of 200 small boats to carry the soldiers through the streams and rivers of Maine.

In mid-September, Arnold set off for Maine with about 1,000 troops. Almost immediately, the regiment faced obstacles. The boats were badly constructed and leaked. Trying to paddle the boats upriver was difficult and exhausting. Whenever they reached rapids or waterfalls, the men had to carry the boats on their backs. The going was rough, and Arnold worried about their slow progress.

Despite the difficulties, Arnold maintained a positive attitude with his troops. Many commanders would have stayed at the rear of the regiment, letting their soldiers forge a path ahead. But not Benedict Arnold. He stayed at the forefront, often waking before dawn to scout the best way forward. As they marched, he would go up and down the line, encouraging the weak and tired troops. When many men fell ill from drinking bad water, he helped organize a makeshift hospital.

In October, early snow began to fall. Food supplies dwindled. Arnold knew his troops would not last without food. He led a small group to search for signs of civilization and find food. In the meantime, Colonel Roger Enos, an officer in charge of one detachment, decided to turn his troops around and go back to Cambridge. Worse, they took a large portion of provisions with them. The rest of the regiment was left to starve.

Arnold returned with food and supplies just in time to save 650 of his men. Ever determined, he allowed the troops to rest for just two days before continuing onward to Quebec City. On December 31, Arnold and his troops attacked Quebec City. He didn't have enough troops to succeed in the attack, but Arnold's army continued to surround the city through the winter and spring before retreating. The plan to take Quebec City was ultimately unsuccessful. But Benedict Arnold had succeeded in leading a dangerous and grueling military expedition. He never gave up and always looked out for his soldiers.

COURAGEOUS BATTLEFIELD HERO

Benedict Arnold was not only an inspiring leader. He also showed bravery on the battlefield. In April 1777, about 4,000 British troops were moving toward Danbury, Connecticut. Danbury was the site of a large patriot arsenal of weapons and ammunition. The British hoped to destroy the town and seize the patriots' weapons.

Arnold knew he needed to rush to Danbury's defense. He and General David Wooster hastily gathered as many militiamen as they could. With only about 500 men, they set off to protect Danbury against thousands of British troops. But they were too late. The British had already attacked the town and were retreating.

General David Wooster

Arnold and Wooster attacked anyway in what became known as the Battle of Ridgefield. In the attack, Wooster suffered a fatal wound. The outnumbered Continental troops began to flee. But Arnold didn't. He rode furiously among his soldiers. Musket balls flew around him. British soldiers took aim and fired, hitting Arnold's horse. The horse fell, thrashing about. Arnold's leg was trapped below the horse. As he desperately tried to break free, a British soldier ran toward him, demanding he surrender. Just in time, Arnold pulled his leg free and shot the redcoat.

The patriot militia dispersed, but Arnold wasn't about to give up. He rallied the troops to ambush the British as they continued south. The British caught wind of the plan and changed their route. Arnold and his militia chased after them. Arnold was again caught in a volley of fire. His horse was shot out from under him yet again, but Arnold rose and continued to fight.

Despite Arnold's valor, skill, and ambition, those in Congress were slow to recognize his accomplishments. When they finally did, it was too late. Benedict Arnold, a patriot hero, was turning traitor.

CHAPTER TWO
A MAN OF LEGEND AND MYTH

Since the time of his treason, Benedict Arnold has remained a reviled, hated figure in the United States. He is probably the most despised Revolutionary player, and for good reason. He betrayed the patriot cause and turned against those who once served under him. But some could argue that he is also misunderstood. General Nathanael Greene described Benedict Arnold as "loved by none, hated by all. Once his country's idol, now her horror." Poems were written about his villainous ways and printed in newspapers. Stories sprang up about his wicked character and evil doings. But not all the stories were true. Some became myths that have stuck through the centuries.

A PROBLEM CHILD?

One myth about Benedict Arnold was that he was an uncontrollable, cruel, and violent youth. As the story goes, one of Arnold's amusements was to rob birds' nests. He loved to mangle young birds in sight of their mothers, and he took delight in the mothers' angry squawks. He enjoyed destroying insects, mutilating toads, and torturing animals. Another story was that he spread broken glass along the path leading from the school so schoolchildren would cut their feet. These tales painted Arnold as a mean-spirited boy—a villain since the days of his youth.

But are these stories true? Little evidence survives about Arnold's early life. Most of the stories came about after Arnold had turned traitor. Likely, the stories were invented to provide a reason for Arnold's treason. Surely no good-hearted person would betray his country, people reasoned. He must have been evil even as a child.

Another myth of Arnold's youth is that he ran away from his apprenticeship to join the militia. As the story goes, in 1758, during the French and Indian War, Arnold bolted from his apprenticeship to join a New York militia, lured by bonus money. He deserted a year later. Some versions say he left because he was bored. Other versions say he left because his mother was dying, and he wanted to be by her side.

But this story falls apart when the facts are examined more closely. The Benedict Arnold in question may have been another youth named "Benedick Arnold."

Records show that Benedick Arnold listed his residence as Norwalk, Connecticut—not Norwich, Connecticut, where Benedict was from. He listed his occupation as weaver, not apothecary. And finally, Benedick Arnold was described as tall. Benedict Arnold was average height. So, the deserter was likely a different Arnold altogether.

A SON OF LIBERTY

Another long-standing myth is that Benedict Arnold turned traitor because he hated America. This is not true. In fact, Arnold was a fervent patriot even before the Revolutionary War began, engaging in acts of resistance against British laws.

In 1765, the Stamp Act required that stamped papers were necessary for all cargo shipped in and out of colonial ports. Benedict Arnold, like many merchants of the time, ignored the requirement. They believed the tax hurt their livelihood as well the economy of port towns. Arnold often snuck past customs officials without paying the duty. In January 1766, a mariner named Peter Boles threatened to report Arnold's actions unless Arnold paid him extra. Arnold refused, and Boles went to the customs office and told on Arnold. When Arnold learned of Boles's tattling, he and a group of men dragged Boles out of a tavern and gave him a beating. Arnold and the others were later arrested and fined. Arnold defended himself in the *Connecticut Gazette* newspaper. He wrote that "trade . . . is nearly ruined by the late detestable Stamp and other oppressive acts . . ."

As the British began passing more tax laws, the colonists got angrier. Around the colonies, rebellious groups formed called The Sons of Liberty. They were most active in Boston. To put down any rebellious activities, the British sent soldiers to patrol the streets of Boston. Bostonians often heckled the patrolling soldiers. Then, on March 5, 1770, a brawl broke out between civilians and the soldiers. Gunfire erupted, and the soldiers fired into the crowd, killing five people. The incident became known as the Boston Massacre.

No one knows who fired the first shots of the Boston Massacre.

Benedict Arnold was on a trading voyage in the West Indies when he heard about the massacre. He was shocked by the "cruel, wanton, and inhuman murders" as he called them. "Are the Americans all asleep and tamely giving up their liberties?" he wrote angrily. If colonists didn't stand up for their rights, he said, "we shall soon see ourselves as poor and as much oppressed as ever."

As war approached, Arnold became the leader of the New Haven militia. He maintained his patriotism throughout the early years of the war. In 1777, even as he was passed over for promotion, he wrote to George Washington of his "zeal for the happiness and safety of my country, in whose cause I have repeatedly fought and bled, and am ready at all times to risk my life."

In 1778, all officers were required to sign an oath of allegiance to the United States of America. Benedict Arnold willingly signed. Although he would break his oath by 1780, Arnold never truly hated America. His reasons for his treachery stemmed from personal frustration with the Continental Congress and the lack of recognition for his sacrifices.

PEGGY THE SPY

One misconception about Arnold's life is that his wife, Peggy Shippen, made him change sides. She certainly played a role in his betrayal, but she wasn't the only reason for it.

In June 1778, after Arnold was wounded in battle, he was made military governor of Philadelphia. Philadelphia had been the headquarters of the British army for nine months until it retreated to New York City. Philadelphia was now the seat of the Continental Congress, but there were still plenty of loyalists in the city.

In Philadelphia, Arnold met and married Peggy Shippen. She was the daughter of a loyalist judge. Arnold was happily married, but he had financial troubles. The Continental Army hadn't paid any of the officers for more than two years because they had run out of money. This added to Arnold's growing disappointment with patriot leadership. In 1779, he began hearing about British offers to pay patriots willing to change sides. So he reached out to Joseph Stansbury, a loyalist merchant. Arnold told him of his willingness to be of service to the British. Stansbury relayed the message to General Henry Clinton. Arnold's primary point of contact would be British spy chief, Major John André.

No one knows the full extent of the role Peggy played in Arnold's decision. Arnold likely spoke to her about his frustrations and lack of faith for the rebel cause. She may have been the one to put him in contact with Stansbury. And, before meeting Arnold, Peggy had become friends with John André. Even after André left Philadelphia, the two had continued to communicate. Her friendship with André may have influenced Arnold to take part in the conspiracy.

Peggy Shippen Arnold had four sons and one daughter, Sophia.

It is certainly true that Peggy helped her husband conspire against the United States. She operated as a go-between. In 1780, Arnold took command of West Point, an important U.S. fort complex. His goal was to turn the fort over to the British. Peggy stayed behind for a time in Philadelphia. André and Stansbury sent her coded letters, which she would then send on to Arnold. Arnold, too, sent coded letters to Peggy with messages for the British. That way, if the letters were intercepted, they would seem like innocent communication between husband and wife.

Just weeks before the treasonous plot was uncovered, Peggy joined Arnold at West Point. The Arnolds were at home when Benedict learned that John André had been captured. Benedict raced upstairs to tell Peggy, and then he fled toward the HMS *Vulture*. Peggy stayed behind, claiming her innocence.

Once Arnold was safely away, Peggy played her final role in the plot. She put on an act of insanity to distract the Continental officers staying in their house. She hoped to buy time for her husband's escape. Peggy opened the bedroom door, shrieking wildly, and ran up and down the hallway. She accused Colonel Varick of ordering her baby to be killed. The confused Varick tried to calm her. When George Washington arrived, she demanded to see him. Washington, who by then knew that Arnold was complicit in the plot to take West Point, went to see her. She was still crying and screaming hysterically. Washington was convinced by her acting, believing she had played no part in the spy ring.

In a letter to Washington, Benedict Arnold wrote that Peggy was "as good and innocent as an angel, and is incapable of doing wrong." He asked that Washington protect Peggy, and Washington did so, still believing Peggy was innocent. He ordered that guards escort Peggy and her child to Philadelphia.

Although Peggy may have spurred Arnold's decision to commit treason, she was not the only reason. His reasons were far more complex. Arnold was bitter that he had been passed over for promotion many times, despite his heroic actions and keen strategies. Additionally, when Arnold was serving as military governor of Philadelphia, a patriot named Joseph Reed began questioning Arnold's expenses. Several charges were brought against him. Arnold maintained his innocence, but he was found guilty of two charges. The first was allowing an enemy ship to dock at a U.S. harbor, and the second was using military wagons for his own personal use. Arnold took the charges as a personal slight.

Meanwhile, the British were giving him recognition that he'd never received from the Americans. A loyalist newspaper called Arnold "an officer more distinguished for valor and perseverance" than any other U.S. commander. It made sense to Arnold to turn his allegiance to the British, with or without Peggy's influence. His wife was just one of many reasons for him to change sides.

LIFE AFTER TREASON

One final misconception is that Arnold got away with treason unscathed. Although he was never formally punished, he did suffer for his actions for the rest of his life.

After Arnold defected, he was given a commission from the British army. But it was far less than the original offer, because the West Point plot had failed. He went on

After switching sides, Benedict Arnold led several small attacks for the British, including a raid in Connecticut.

to lead British troops until 1781, when Lord Cornwallis took over.

Arnold returned to British headquarters in New York. He offered military advice to British General Clinton, but his advice was ignored time and again. Had Clinton listened, the British might have won the war, but in the end the patriots came out victorious. After the war, Arnold moved to London and tried to get a position with the British East India Company. He was turned down because the general public distrusted him.

In 1785, feeling shunned by the British, Arnold moved his family to New Brunswick, Canada, where he began a trading business. The family stayed there for several years. But the Canadian economy floundered because of the ongoing war between Great Britain and France. His business dreams shattered, Arnold and his family returned to London in 1791. Arnold tried to enlist in the war against the French, but he had proven himself untrustworthy. Suspicious military members rejected him.

Arnold struggled to keep his trading business alive, but he was deeply in debt. He remained in debt for the rest of his life. His great-nephew Isaac N. Benedict wrote that, at the end of his life, Arnold's "bitter disappointments, cares and embarrassments [. . .] pressed heavily upon [him]." Benedict Arnold died on June 14, 1801, and was buried without military honors.

CHAPTER THREE
SAD TRUTHS

*B*enedict Arnold was a man of accomplishments and a legendary traitor. Myths abound about the general, but there are also some lesser-known truths.

A FRIENDSHIP BETRAYED

Prior to his betrayal, Benedict Arnold and George Washington had been friends. Given the direct impact Arnold's betrayal had on Washington, this fact may surprise some people.

Washington and Arnold were different in many ways. Washington was tall and reserved in his manner and speech. Arnold was smaller, fiery, and animated. But the two were alike in their zeal for the American cause. Washington often called Arnold his "fighting general."

Benedict Arnold met Washington for the first time in August 1775. Washington had just been named commander-in-chief of the Continental Army. Arnold wished to meet with him to express his desire to lead an expedition to Quebec, Canada. Washington had heard about Arnold and his success in the capture of Fort Ticonderoga. Upon their first meeting, Washington was impressed by Arnold's passion for the cause. He was even more impressed when Arnold submitted a written plan for marching through the Maine wilderness and taking Quebec. He agreed that Arnold should lead the Quebec campaign. Although the Americans ultimately failed to seize Quebec City, Arnold's march through the wilderness impressed Washington. He wrote to Arnold, saying, "Many thanks are due, and sincerely offered to you, for your enterprising and persevering spirit."

Throughout the early years of the war, Washington supported and endorsed Arnold, even when other military leaders and Congress doubted Arnold. In February 1777, Congress passed over Arnold for promotion to major general. Washington wrote to Arnold, saying he would "remedy any error" and, fearful that Arnold would resign, begged him to remain in the army. He then wrote to Congress, stating that "Surely a more active, a more spirited, and sensible officer, fills no department in your army."

Arnold, meanwhile, considered resigning. As he was preparing to return to civilian life, he received word that

George Washington led the patriot forces to victory against the British and his former friend Benedict Arnold in 1783.

the British army was marching toward Danbury to seize patriot weapons. He acted swiftly, and his valor on the battlefield was eventually rewarded with a promotion to major general. But he was still considered a junior officer to those who'd been promoted before him. Washington met with Arnold, imploring him to remain in the army and forget about rank for the time being. British troops had recaptured Fort Ticonderoga, and Washington feared they would continue making progress. He needed Benedict Arnold's strategy and leadership. Perhaps out of loyalty to his friend, Arnold agreed not to resign.

Throughout the war, Washington and Arnold exchanged much correspondence. Although their letters were usually focused on the war and military strategy, the two occasionally inquired about each other's personal well-being and health. In March 1777, Arnold heard that Washington had been ill, and wrote that he was worried that Washington would "exert yourself, before you are perfectly recovered." Later, after Arnold was injured at the Battle of Breymann's Redoubt, Washington wrote to express his concern, saying "There is none who wishes more sincerely" for Arnold to be on his feet again.

The friendship between Washington and Arnold makes Arnold's betrayal all the worse. Arnold gave the British information on Washington's whereabouts, so the British could capture him. It could have led to Washington's death. So what happened to bring about the ruin of their friendship?

One factor was Arnold's court-martial in Philadelphia in 1779. Arnold claimed to be innocent. But he was found guilty on two counts of misusing his military authority. His sentence was to be an official reprimand from George Washington. Arnold held out hope that Washington would ignore the court's findings, but that was not the case. Washington issued a public reprimand, calling Arnold's actions "reprehensible" and "imprudent and improper." Washington also wrote a private letter to Arnold. The letter was gently worded, praising Arnold's accomplishments, while also scolding him.

By this time, Arnold had already begun secret correspondence with the British, but Washington's reprimand was another blow. He felt that the commander who had supported him throughout his career was now bowing to political pettiness and turning against him. Arnold felt he had no one on his side. So he turned completely against his country and commander.

Washington discovered Arnold's betrayal on the morning of September 25, 1780. He read through the papers discovered in Major John André's boot and realized what Arnold, his friend and valued general, had done. Hands shaking, Washington grasped the treasonous papers and bowed his head. "Arnold has betrayed me," he said. "Whom can we trust now?" His words were a sad ending to a trusted friendship.

Head Quarters middle
Brook April 20th 1779

259

Sir,

I am honored with yours of the 12th.
Instant with the several Resolves of Congress refer-
red to, inclosed — to which I shall pay due attention
and obedience. I have appointed the 1st of May for
the Court Martial to sit for the trial of Major General
Arnold, of which I have given notice to the President
and Council of the State of Pennsylvania and
to the General —

I have the honor to be
with great respect
Your most Obet. Servt.
Go Washington

John Jay Esqr.
Presidt of Congress

George Washington wrote a letter to fellow founding father John Jay
regarding Benedict Arnold's court-martial.

A DISAPPEARED HERO

Another lesser-known fact is that Benedict Arnold was fully erased from all military records. The name of the heroic, brilliant, and strategic general whose accomplishments helped the United States win the war disappeared from military accounts as if he'd never existed.

After Arnold's treachery was discovered, Washington ordered Alexander Hamilton and military officer James McHenry to find and arrest Arnold. The two men leapt onto their horses and galloped after Arnold. But they were too late. Arnold had already safely boarded the British HMS *Vulture*.

Onboard the *Vulture*, Arnold wrote a letter to Washington justifying his actions. He stated, "I have ever acted from a principle of love to my country, since the commencement of the present unhappy contest between Great Britain and the colonies, the same principle of love to my country actuates my present conduct, however it may appear inconsistent to the world: who very seldom judge right of any man's actions."

Washington, though, felt the betrayal was deeply personal. He had defended Arnold from those who had questioned his abilities. He'd overlooked Arnold's questionable behavior and expenses. And now Arnold had done the unthinkable by betraying his country. Washington was angry. He called Arnold a villain, and said he was "lost to all sense of honour and shame."

At West Point, one of the main forts had been named Fort Arnold in honor of Benedict Arnold. Immediately, the name was changed to Fort Clinton.

As word spread about Arnold's treason, an angry mob rushed into the cemetery in Norwich, Connecticut, Arnold's hometown. The mob destroyed his father's and infant brother's gravestones. In New Milford, Connecticut, a crowd paraded figures of Arnold and Satan through the streets.

George Washington initially offered to exchange Major John André for Arnold, but British General

Clinton refused. Then Washington approved a plan to kidnap Arnold from New York City, ordering that Arnold should be taken alive, wanting to make a public example of him. Washington later changed his mind about keeping Arnold alive, instead ordering that he be executed on the spot if he was caught.

On October 4, 1780, Congress ordered the Board of War to erase Arnold's name from its official rolls and reports. Despite Arnold's many contributions to the Revolutionary War, he would never receive official recognition for his role.

Angry Americans in New Milford, Connecticut, created a likeness of Benedict Arnold being controlled by the devil.

In Saratoga National Historical Park, near the site of Breymann's Redoubt, a gray granite marker stands. On one side of the marker, a battered boot is carved. The other side reads, "In memory of the most brilliant soldier of the Continental Army, who was desperately wounded on this spot, the sally port of Burgoyne's Great Western Redoubt, 7th October 1777, winning for his countrymen the decisive battle of the American Revolution and for himself the rank of Major General."

This "brilliant soldier" was none other than Benedict Arnold. But his name does not appear on the stone at all.

Benedict Arnold's name is purposely missing from the monument at Saratoga National Historical Park.

PRISON ESCAPE

Benedict Arnold was never formally punished for his crime of treason. But one little-known fact is that he was imprisoned briefly, long after the Revolutionary War.

In 1794, Arnold was making his living by trading in the West Indies. The island of Guadeloupe, once controlled by the French, was now occupied by the British. When Arnold made his way to Guadeloupe's port, Pointe-a-Pitre, he didn't realize the French had seized the island from the British. As he sailed into the port, he saw that the ships were French. He decided to land anyway.

When the French questioned him, Arnold gave a fake name—John Anderson—and said that he was an American merchant. The French were suspicious, though, and arrested him as a British spy. He was taken to a French prison ship in the harbor.

On the prison ship, Arnold bribed the guards to give him information. They told him that the French governor had discovered his real identity and was about to hang him. They also told him that a British fleet had arrived to blockade the harbor.

With a British ship in the harbor, Arnold saw his chance to escape. He bribed the guards again to position a raft near the ship. When the tide went out, Arnold placed his money in a cask and dropped it overboard. Then he slithered out the cabin window, slid down a rope, and dropped onto the raft. With his hands, he paddled to a rowboat, leapt aboard, and rowed hard toward the British ship, the *Boyne*. A small French vessel chased after him, but Arnold outmaneuvered it. He made it safely to the *Boyne*. Once again, with a bit of luck, Arnold had escaped punishment and death.

CHAPTER FOUR
ARNOLD'S DOWNFALLS

$\mathcal{B}$enedict Arnold was a brilliant general, and he had many positive traits. He was ambitious, often generous, and passionate. But he also had faults that ultimately led to his downfall. He was outspoken, stubborn, and proud. He often clashed with his superiors and was difficult to get along with. These character traits earned him a long list of bitter enemies.

ENEMIES AND RIVALS

One of Arnold's first enemies was Ethan Allen, leader of the Green Mountain Boys. After Arnold and Allen took Fort Ticonderoga, the two shared command of the fort. Arnold was disgusted by the rowdiness of the Green Mountain Boys, who drank a lot and were disrespectful toward him. When Arnold tried to discipline the Boys,

The Americans may not have won the Battle of Ticonderoga if not for the leadership of Benedict Arnold, though he was given little credit for it.

Allen scolded him and insisted on his right to command the fort. In his report to Congress, Allen took credit for taking Fort Ticonderoga. Congress, believing Arnold to be rash and disagreeable, stripped him of his command. Arnold seethed with anger. He didn't like the idea of being second in command. So he resigned his post.

After the march to Quebec City in late 1775, Arnold and his troops surrounded the city to cut it off from supplies. In the spring of 1776, Arnold proposed launching a surprise attack on Fort Anne in Canada. Colonel Moses Hazen criticized the plan as being reckless and foolish. The Continental Army eventually withdrew from Canada, and several officers went to Philadelphia. There they asked Congress to investigate Arnold. During the hearings, the officers criticized Arnold's command decisions and his rash orders. The charges against Arnold were eventually dismissed, but his reputation was scarred.

General Horatio Gates, who admired Benedict Arnold, was astonished by the charges and wrote in support of Arnold. He elevated Arnold to commander of the patriot fleet on Lake Champlain. But Gates and Arnold eventually became enemies as well.

In September 1777, Arnold was serving under Gates in Saratoga. Gates was a cautious general who often waited to be attacked rather than attacking first. Arnold, on the other hand, had more aggressive ideas. He tried to persuade Gates to attack the approaching British. Gates refused. The two argued bitterly. Gates banned Arnold from strategy meetings and put other officers in charge of some of Arnold's troops.

Eventually, Gates allowed Arnold to ride out with a small regiment, which resulted in the Battle of Freeman's Farm. There the patriots slowed the British troops' forward progress. Gates took credit for the battle in his

American General Horatio Gates (center) oversaw the surrender of British troops at Saratoga on October 17, 1777.

reports. Arnold was incensed, and he and Gates argued again. Gates ordered him to leave but Arnold refused. In October, Arnold defied Gates's orders to stay in camp and rode into the midst of the Second Battle of Saratoga.

Although Arnold's strategies were often the right moves to take, his defiance and aggressive tendencies made him many enemies. His eventual betrayal and treason seemed to prove his enemies right.

A SELFISH TRAITOR

Benedict Arnold's biggest flaw was his decision to betray the patriot cause. Although he had several reasons, ultimately his decision was self-serving.

In 1779, Arnold began secretly negotiating with the British. Outwardly he pretended to be committed to American independence. He continued to correspond with George Washington and other officers, faking his commitment to the revolution.

Arnold's main point of contact in the British spy ring was Major John André. The two communicated using secret code and invisible ink. The correspondence went on for more than a year. Eventually, Arnold and the British hatched a plan. Arnold would assume command of West Point, an important U.S. fort complex in New York. He would then give the British a detailed plan of the fort. If the British could take control of West Point, the rebellion would likely be squashed.

In 1780, General Washington asked Arnold to take command of an entire wing of the army. It was a position that Arnold would have appreciated early in the war. But he refused, asking instead for command of West Point. Washington agreed.

West Point is located in the bluffs surrounding the Hudson River.

Benedict Arnold (right) met John André (left) under cover of darkness on September 22, 1780.

In September 1780, Arnold was installed as the West Point commander. He and André arranged to meet in person to go over the details of how to turn West Point over to the British. At midnight on September 22, the two met in the woods along the Hudson River. They talked long into the night.

When André and Arnold came back to the river, they saw that André's escape boat was gone. Arnold took André to a trusted friend, Joshua Hett Smith. The plan was that André would later slip away to a British ship, the HMS *Vulture*. But while at Smith's, the men heard the Continentals fire on the *Vulture*. The ship was retreating.

Arnold knew he had to get André out of patriot territory. He wrote André a pass. He also wrote several pages describing the fort as well as George Washington's whereabouts. André slipped the plans into his boot, changed out of his British uniform, and tried to escape across British lines.

Along the way, André was stopped by Continental militiamen. He showed them his pass, but the soldiers were suspicious. They searched him, found the papers in his boot, and captured him.

Three colonial militiamen captured André.

Arnold heard about the arrest on the morning of September 25, as he was waiting for General Washington to arrive at West Point. He knew he would be implicated in the plot. He had to leave immediately. He raced to shore, boarded a barge, and ordered the crew to take him to the HMS *Vulture* downriver.

After his treason was discovered, Arnold showed little remorse. He wrote to Washington, asking him to spare John André's life, with a warning that a "torrent of blood . . . may be spilt in consequence" if André was executed. Despite Arnold's threat, André was hanged on October 2, 1780.

After his betrayal, Arnold officially became a British general. In a letter to the American people, published in the *Royal Gazette* in New York, Arnold tried to justify his actions, although he remained unapologetic. He blamed France's involvement in the war, saying that he found it wiser to place his faith in the British rather than the French monarchy, which he called an "enemy of the Protestant faith." He went on to say that he was dedicating himself to the "reunion of the British empire as the best and only means to dry up the streams of misery that have deluged this country." He also urged Americans to side with the British, a sure sign that he'd turned his back on the patriot cause.

CHAPTER FIVE
REDEEMING ACHIEVEMENT

*B*enedict Arnold's legacy is mixed. He is remembered as a traitor. But his legacy would be incomplete without recognizing his military achievements. Without Benedict Arnold's leadership and strategies, the United States may not have won the Revolutionary War.

Benedict Arnold's strategies early in the war had significant impacts. The capture of Fort Ticonderoga in 1775 established a Continental presence in the north. The following year, the Battle of Valcour Island slowed down the British advance. But America suffered many losses as well. In 1776, the British effectively captured New York City, establishing it as their headquarters. The British also took New Jersey, pushing the Continental Army back into Pennsylvania. The war, to many Americans, seemed never-ending. That is, until the Battles of Saratoga in September and October 1777.

In September 1777, Arnold was stationed near Saratoga, New York, under the command of General Horatio Gates. Gates made no move as the British, under General John Burgoyne, approached. He wanted to wait until the British attacked. Arnold argued against that. He finally convinced Gates to let him and a small regiment ride out and determine the redcoats' numbers. A furious battle ensued on a stretch of land known as Freeman's Farm. Gates refused to send more men to Arnold's side. Because of that, the regiment was unable to stop the British from continuing their march south. But the patriots had slowed Burgoyne's progress.

After the battle, many soldiers heaped admiration and praise on Arnold for his actions. Even British General Burgoyne acknowledged Arnold's role. But Gates decided to take the credit for the battle. In his reports to Congress, he didn't mention Arnold's name. Instead, he made it sound as though he had been the one to take action.

In October 1777, the Second Battle of Saratoga raged near Bemis Heights. Arnold defied Gates's orders to stay in camp and rode out into the midst of the battle. The Continental soldiers, buoyed by Arnold's appearance, fought on. The British retreated.

But Arnold was not finished. He turned toward Breymann's Redoubt, a small fortification held by the British. He rode into the fort and raised his sword, signaling his men to charge. Then the surprised British fired. Arnold's horse went down and landed on his leg.

The injury was serious. Arnold spent months recovering in a hospital. Meanwhile, at Saratoga, General Burgoyne surrendered his entire army of 6,000 men. Arnold's actions had effectively stopped Burgoyne's forward march. But General Gates took all the glory, leaving none for Arnold. Congress gave Gates a gold medal.

Most historians point to the Battles of Saratoga as the turning point of the war. With Burgoyne's surrender, the British lost all hope of holding the Hudson Valley.

News of the major Continental victory caught the attention of one of Great Britain's oldest enemies—the country of France. Great Britain and France had fought numerous wars over the centuries. Great Britain's defeat of France in the Seven Years' War increased the bitterness between the two countries. Since 1776, American

Arnold was wounded when his horse was shot out from under him at the Second Battle of Saratoga.

diplomat Benjamin Franklin had been working with France to form an alliance. He urged the French to support American efforts at independence.

The victory at Saratoga encouraged France to formally enter the war. The French realized that it was possible for the American rebels to win, and they knew the new country would be an important ally. With the 1778 Treaty of Alliance, France officially recognized the United States as an independent country. Great Britain then declared war on France.

France's involvement in the war was vital to the patriots' success. The French sent troops and ships to North America. And France also supplied the patriots with funding. The financial and military support was just what the Continental Congress needed to bolster the war effort. Additionally, now that Britain and France were officially at war again, the conflict spread to other areas of the world. The British had to split their attentions. They could no longer just focus on the war in North America.

The Continental forces may not have won the victory at Saratoga without the foresight, strategy, and aggressive tactics of Benedict Arnold. And, without the victory at Saratoga, France may not have entered the war. Benedict Arnold deserves credit for his role in paving the way toward independence.

Arnold's military leadership wasn't the only way he led the patriots to victory. His treason actually helped them win the war as well.

France's involvement in the war in 1778 did not immediately end the conflict. The war continued to drag on. American citizens and soldiers alike suffered. Food was rationed. Soldiers were rarely paid, if at all. Many Americans were beginning to wonder if the struggle for independence was worth the effort.

The discovery of Benedict Arnold's treason in 1780 changed Americans' minds. They were shocked that one of their own generals, once so loyal, had turned against the patriots' cause. Worse, he'd tried to bring about Continental defeat and the capture of their beloved commander-in-chief, General George Washington. If Arnold had been successful in his plot, the British could have won, and the revolution would have been over. This realization renewed colonial fervor for the war and independence.

One year later, the patriots achieved victory. In October 1781, Lord Cornwallis surrendered his force of more than 7,000 to General Washington in the Battle of Yorktown, Virginia. Although some fighting still took place, it was the last big battle of the Revolutionary War. The war officially ended with the Treaty of Paris in 1783.

Benedict Arnold's name will forever be linked to the Revolutionary War. His heroic efforts helped the American patriots achieve many victories. Ultimately, though, his decision to betray the fight for independence made him what he is known as today—a traitor.

TIMELINE

JANUARY 14, 1741
Benedict Arnold is born in Norwich, Connecticut.

1755
Arnold begins his apprenticeship at his relatives' apothecary shop.

1761
Arnold opens his own business in New Haven, Connecticut.

1774
Arnold organizes a unit of militiamen in New Haven.

MAY 1775
Arnold co-leads the capture of Fort Ticonderoga, New York.

SEPTEMBER 1775
Arnold leads an expedition through the Maine wilderness to
Quebec City, Canada.

OCTOBER 1776
Arnold participates in the Battle of Valcour Island, delaying the
British advance.

FEBRUARY 1777
Arnold is passed over for promotion to major general.

APRIL 1777
Arnold leads his troops in the Battle of Ridgefield.

MAY 1777
Arnold is promoted to major general although he does not have
seniority over those promoted before him.

SEPTEMBER–OCTOBER 1777
Arnold suffers a leg injury in the Second Battle of Saratoga.

JUNE 1778
George Washington names Arnold military governor of Philadelphia, Pennsylvania.

APRIL 8, 1779
Benedict Arnold marries Peggy Shippen.

AUGUST 1780
George Washington gives Arnold command of West Point. Arnold plans to turn the fort over to the British.

SEPTEMBER 22, 1780
Arnold meets with British spy Major John André and gives him detailed plans of West Point.

SEPTEMBER 23, 1780
John André is stopped and searched by American soldiers. They find the West Point plans and arrest him.

SEPTEMBER 25, 1780
Arnold learns of André's capture and escapes to a British warship.

1781
Arnold leads British troops in combat against the Americans.

OCTOBER 19, 1781
British General Cornwallis surrenders to George Washington at Yorktown, signaling the end of the war.

JUNE 14, 1801
Benedict Arnold dies in London, England.

GLOSSARY

apothecary—person who made and sold medicines

apprentice—a person who is learning a trade or art by experience under a skilled worker

arsenal—a storehouse of weapons and ammunition

blockade—the cutting off of an area by means of troops or warships to stop people or supplies from coming in or going out

channel—a narrow waterway between two areas of land

commandeer—to take by military force

conspiracy—the act of working together secretly to do something unlawful

defect—to desert a cause or party to take up another

implicate—to show someone is involved in a criminal matter

loyalist—an American colonist who remained loyal to the British during the Revolutionary War

mariner—a person who directs or helps to navigate a ship

merchant—a buyer and seller of goods for profit

militia—a body of citizens with some military training who are called to active duty only during an emergency

Parliament—a legislative body of government

port—a harbor or city where ships load or unload cargo

reprimand—a severe or formal criticism

sally port—a gateway permitting the passage of a large number of troops at a time

FURTHER READING

Castrovilla, Selene. *Revolutionary Rogues: John André and Benedict Arnold.* Honesdale, PA: Calkins Creek, 2017.

Derr, Aaron. *Benedict Arnold: Hero or Enemy Spy?* Egremont, MA: Red Chair Press, 2018.

Loh-Hagan, Virginia. *The Real Benedict Arnold.* Ann Arbor, MI: 45th Parallel Press, 2018.

INTERNET SITES

Benedict Arnold
kids.britannica.com/kids/article/Benedict-Arnold/489795

Benedict Arnold Biography
academickids.com/encyclopedia/index.php/Benedict_Arnold

Benedict Arnold Biography for Kids
www.mrnussbaum.com/benedict-arnold/

SOURCE NOTES

Page 22, "loved by none..." Nathaniel Philbrick. *Valiant Ambition: George Washington, Benedict Arnold, and the Fate of the American Revolution*. New York: Viking Press, 2016, p. 594.

Page 25, "trade...is nearly..." James Kirby Martin. *Benedict Arnold, Revolutionary Hero: An American Warrior Reconsidered*. New York: New York University Press, 1997, p. 45.

Page 26, "cruel, wanton..." Ibid., p. 58.

Page 26, "zeal for..." Willard Sterne Randall. *Benedict Arnold: Patriot and Traitor*. New York: William Morrow, 1990, p. 329.

Page 29, "as good and innocent..." Ibid., p. 560.

Page 30, "an officer..." Ibid., p. 453.

Page 32, "bitter disappointment..." Jim Murphy. *The Real Benedict Arnold*. New York: Houghton Mifflin, 2007, p. 232.

Page 34, "Many thanks are due..." *Benedict Arnold, Revolutionary Hero: An American Warrior Reconsidered*, p. 184.

Page 34, "remedy any error..." Ibid., p. 308.

Page 36, "exert yourself..." Benedict Arnold, "To George Washington from Brigadier General Benedict Arnold, 26 March 1777," founders.archives.gov/documents/Washington/03-08-02-0688, Accessed April 9, 2019.

Page 36, "There is none..." Ibid., Accessed April 9, 2019.

Page 37, "reprehensible" *Benedict Arnold: Patriot and Traitor*, p. 494.

Page 37, "imprudent and improper," Ibid., p. 494.

Page 37, "Arnold has betrayed..." Ibid., p. 558.

Page 39, "I have ever acted..." Benedict Arnold, "To George Washington from Benedict Arnold, 25 September 1780," founders.archives.gov/documents/Washington/99-01-02-03372, Accessed April 9, 2019.

Page 39, "lost to all..." *Benedict Arnold: Patriot and Traitor*, p. 564.

Page 51, "torrent of blood..." Arnold, Benedict, "To George Washington from Benedict Arnold, 1 October 1780," founders. archives.gov/documents/Washington/99-01-02-03451, Accessed April 9, 2019.

Page 51, "enemy of..." *Benedict Arnold: Patriot and Traitor*, p. 575.

SELECT BIBLIOGRAPHY

Benedict Arnold
www.mountvernon.org/library/digitalhistory/digital-encyclopedia/article/benedict-arnold/

Benedict Arnold: A Traitor, but Once a Patriot
www.usnews.com/news/national/articles/2008/06/27/benedict-arnold-a-traitor-but-once-a-patriot

Benedict Arnold, Revolutionary Hero
www.mountvernon.org/george-washington/the-revolutionary-war/george-washington-benedict-arnold/

Martin, James Kirby. *Benedict Arnold, Revolutionary Hero: An American Warrior Reconsidered*. New York: New York University Press, 1997.

Murphy, Jim. *The Real Benedict Arnold*. New York: Houghton Mifflin, 2007.

Philbrick, Nathaniel. *Valiant Ambition: George Washington, Benedict Arnold, and the Fate of the American Revolution*. New York: Viking Press, 2016.

Randall, Willard Sterne. *Benedict Arnold: Patriot and Traitor*. New York,: William Morrow, 1990.

INDEX